CW00402811

R.R.P.
£4.95

GREN'S GUIDE TO RUGBY

PUBLISHED BY

WESTERN MAIL & ECHO LTD

THOMSON HOUSE, HAVELOCK STREET, CARDIFF CF1 1XR.
TELEPHONE CARDIFF 01222 583583/223333
Registered Number 46946 England

Designed and typeset by
Andrew Jones, Carol Williams, Louise Baker

Printed by
Mid Wales Litho Ltd, New Inn, Pontypool, Gwent

British Library Cataloguing-in-Publication Data.

A catalogue of this book is available from The National Library of Wales and The British Library.

ISBN 09504042 68

CONTENTS

INTRODUCTION

"In 1823 at Rugby School, young William Webb-Ellis who, with a true disregard for the rules of football, as played in his time, took the ball in his arms and ran with it, thus originating the distinctive feature of The Rugby Game"

So, Rugby was born, and ever since people have been baffled by the game. Wondering why teams of up to fifteen fairly intelligent men and sometimes women, want to knock lumps off another fifteen or so for enjoyment. In the following pages we hope to explain such things.

PLAYING POSITIONS

or where to stand on the field depending upon your shape, size and ability
(don't worry too much about the latter)

THE FULL BACK NO.15

A much-sought-after glamour position beloved by the broad-shouldered, death-or-glory players who enjoy getting involved with the game only when they feel so inclined.

Bursting into the lines is a much-loved tactic often employed by full backs to warm themselves up after cold periods of inactivity. These periods of inactivity are referred to by full backs as tactical covering. The forwards refer to them as "hiding".

Full backs also develop a skill which renders them obstructed by their own team while bravely going for a high ball which is being pursued by at least ten of the opposition psychopaths – after (and this is very important) shouting a very brave, theatrical and entirely misleading "My Ball!"

THE WING THREEQUARTER
(NO.11 AND 14)

To really enjoy a career as a winger you must have three qualities:

    1 speed
    2 indifference to inactivity
    3 be a natural at chatting up the girls who hang around the touchline

Many wingers who talk of their "best games" are not referring to the games in which they played brilliantly, but the games in which they arranged most dates with the opposite sex.

Recently a club winger we know had arranged five separate dates before half-time and during the second half met, and got engaged to, one of the opposition team's travelling groupies.

THE CENTRE THREEQUARTER (NO.12 AND 13)

This position accommodates the most shapely of players. If the centres are stocky (or even fat) they consider themselves to be crash-ball experts. While the slim centres you see delicately offering "hospital passes" are would-be outside halves who can't replace the current incumbent – who is the person most often on the receiving end of his "hospital passes" for obvious reasons.

THE OUTSIDE HALF NO.10

Everyone wants to be the outside half – the player around whom the play is made, the player who dictates the game, the player whose ability decides style and tone of the whole team.

Ideally the outside half should be broad-shouldered, slim-waisted and have a golden mane (Ideal for attracting attention of Selectors – see later chapter)

There are two types of outside half:

1 The kind who kicks ("He kicks too much – hasn't he ever heard of getting his line going?")

2 The running and passing type (Hasn't he ever heard of tactical kicking?")

To really establish yourself at outside half you should ideally be a true athlete, intelligent and related to the chairman of the selection committee.

THE SCRUM HALF NO.9

To be a scrum-half one should be strong, short, have a very low centre of gravity, and also have ability to talk non-stop throughout the game – even when unconscious.

A scrum half never has a bad game. If he should have a stinker, it's not his fault: the forwards gave him rubbish ball and no protection.

If, however, he has a good game it's: "Who couldn't play a blinder behind a pack like that?"

THE PROPS NO.1 AND 3

Props are the hairy ones you see getting up last from a collapsed scrum yet always the first into the club bar after the game.

They happily grunt away the afternoon in the darkness of scrums, rucks and mauls in the hope of providing ball for their backs – all of whom are considered fairies anyway by any self-respecting prop.

THE HOOKER NO.2

The beauty of being a hooker is that you always get a game because very few people actually want to play there.

Most clubs are bursting at the seams with outside halves, wingers, scrum halves and full backs but clubs are lucky if they've got more than one hooker.

Hookers are born and not made. They must have no neck, but bandy legs are essential. And arms that are so long that the knuckles trail along the floor are a great help.

SECOND ROW LOCKS NO.4 AND 5

Locks are big, gangling chaps who are in the team purely to get the retaliation going (and to push, shove and jump now and then).

Props are honest, open thugs – not, for them, the delicate yet sly punch in the loose to which flankers resort. Locks are honest and take pride in a well-delivered blow to an opposition jaw during early line outs. The referee misses these incidents because locks work in tandem – the other one operating as referee attention diverter.

FLANKERS NO.6 AND 7

Flankers are the flash ones of the forwards, running about tackling everyone and generally behaving in a most unfriendly manner.

Flankers tend to bleed a lot and seek sympathy from spectators and refs alike. They also get knocked out a lot and emerge from the medics' grasp swathed in bandages dramatically determined to return to the field of play. They seek the attention of touchline admirers with their "I'm-prepared-to-die-for-this-club" attitude.

THE NUMBER EIGHT NO.8

He's the tallish chap who can be seen leaning on the back of the scrum preventing the ball from coming out quickly – this he considers to be tactics while his scrum half considers it to be just good old-fashioned awkwardness.

Number eights are, of course, frustrated scrum halves. Denied by height from being so, they still do the scrum halves' job by picking up from the back of the scrum and trying to ferret over from five yards or so – and usually fail.

TYPES OF KICK

Although rugby is supposed to be a handling game, kicking plays a very important part in developing attacks, clearing defence, scoring penalty points and smacking the ball (accidentally) into the naughty regions of the opposing team's psychopath.

Kicking is, of course, a very basic natural movement. The ball should be struck with the swinging foot, ideally the foot you're not standing on. If you can kick equally well with either foot why are you reading this book anyway?

THE GRUBBER KICK

This is a low-trajectory kick designed to make the ball bounce and roll tantalisingly towards the touch line before eluding a frustrated defender's grasp as it bobbles into touch.

Well, that at least is the theory – but what usually happens is that the ball is miskicked straight into an opponent's hand, whereupon he runs back at you and the rest of your team to score under the posts for a winning try.

Grubber kicks are best left to people like Rob Andrew or Neil Jenkins.

THE PUNT

This is the frenzied kick so loved by front-row players who much to their horror and amazement, receive the ball in open play.

Unable to run or pass (without being sick) they punt the ball hopefully in the direction of the opposition line. This attitude has been commemorated in Latin by a leading Welsh Valley club whose club emblem is supported by the words "If yer gerrit, kickit".

THE UP AND UNDER

This is something like the punt, but the ball should be kicked much higher, thus giving you and your sadistic group of little friends more time to run forward and trample the poor innocent who is stupid enough to try to catch the landing ball.

Up and unders (or Uppenunders as they are sometimes known) are good fun and should be used as often as possible.

THE TOUCH-FINDING SCREW KICK

In this kick the ball is hit with the outside of the boot. This should send the ball spinning long and parallel to the touch line and eventually it should drift into touch.

Never ever attempt this kick, as you will probably hit it two yards into the stand. Or in the very unlikely event that the kick goes where you intended it to, everyone will think it's a total fluke anyway.

THE CHIP KICK

This is a beautiful short, neat, clever little kick which is used to put the ball just over the heads of an advancing defence in the hope that you or one of your fellow players can catch the ball and make way towards the try line.

This kick when executed correctly is a delight to see – but what you don't see is the advancing opposition's full back, playfully smashing his fist into our hero's ribs as he attempts to go around him in pursuit.

THE DROP KICK

This kick is usually undertaken by the golden-maned outside half, who considers he is the only member of the team capable of such things. In the drop kick, the ball should be struck as it's hitting the ground. If correctly executed the ball will sail high and wide between the posts and you will be considered either a hero for gaining a few points or an idiot for not giving the ball out to the unmarked wing for two more.

THE PLACE KICK

This kick is the only one taken when the ball is stationary. It rests upon the ground, the mound of sand or a plastic tee as our hero goes through his much-rehearsed concentration before he approaches the ball to whack it high and between the posts.

It's worth pointing out that as place kicks, these days, take so long to take, this is a good time for those watching to read the programme, go to the loo, or get another pint from the bar.

THE HACK KICK

This particular kick is mostly used by players who have turned to the joys of rugby, after having played soccer.

With this type of kick the ball is booted in the direction that the player is facing, no matter which way he's playing.

The kick is frowned upon by the "experts" but it's a very useful kick to have in your kicking armoury. Some accomplished users of this kick can every time, with a thunderous whack, wind an opponent from fifteen yards.

TYPES OF PASS

In this chapter we have not covered the more usual type of pass, such as throwing the ball vertically into the air while you scream and run away from that very disagreeable hairy tackler who seems to want the ball more than you do anyway.

Due to space limitations, we have decided to feature the more constructive passes.

PASS TO THE LEFT

Ideally this should be used when the person
to whom you wish to receive the ball is
standing on your left.

PASS TO THE RIGHT

As for passing to the left except it would be
nice if the recipient could be on your right.

THE VARSITY PASS

This is the poseur's pass: a flash, don't-look-and-lob-it-over-your-shoulder pass to be executed when your side is at least thirty points ahead or if you are trying to impress a groupie bird in the stand.

THE REVERSE PASS

Useful during moments of sheer terror or panic (eg when confronted by your girlfriend's husband coming marauding aggressively around the blind side) to change the direction of attack.

THE SMART-ARSE FRENCH PASS

Typical Froggie clever-dick stuff which always seems to work for them, yet if you try it they'll intercept and score.

Never use the French pass unless you're related to the club chairman.

THE DIVE PASS

Mainly used by flash scrum halves when they know they are being watched by country or county selectors. It should be used in dry conditions only, as nothing is more guaranteed to wreck your chances with the touch-line talent than the sight of your delicate artistic dive ending up as an ungraceful belly flop in a muddy pool.

THE SPIN PASS

This pass is beloved by scrum halves because they are totally convinced that a spinning ball travels much further. You can always tell when the spin pass has been used: the ball can be seen spinning off the outside half's chest or his legs, his forehead....

THE DROPPED PASS

This is the most common of all the passes. It requires no skill in execution. Just take your eye off the ball and it happens!

Many wings with no one to beat and the winning try line only yards away employ this pass – it heightens the drama and excites opposition supporters.

THE FLIP PASS

This is the favourite pass of chicken centres who have no desire to be holding the ball when the opposition psychopath is about to pounce.

On the credit side, if from your cowardly flip pass a try is scored you will be considered as having great vision and tactical awareness etc etc

THE HOSPITAL PASS

This pass is thrown so that the recipient gets the ball at exactly the same time as the opposition's stiff-arming, knees-high, kidney-pounding specialist hits you.

This pass should be given away at selected times, for instance, to your wife's boyfriend, or to the guy who stole that girl who you bought all those drinks for on the last Easter tour. You could also be the toast of the squad if you manage to give a hospital pass to the coach when he's playing in one of these gala matches.

RUGBY TERMS EXPLAINED

As with every sport, correct terminology is all important, and, if you aspire to be taken seriously as a rugby person, it's necessary that you understand such terms.

CONVERSION

If it's against your team it's a kick
which will add two undeserved
points to a lucky five.

MARK

A bruised, broken, dented bit of
flesh or bone received while trying
to catch a high ball.

THE LINE-OUT

A touch-line confrontation between both sets of
forwards when the ref insists on a yard between the
two sides before they start punching each other.

FOUL PLAY

An incident seen only by the ref when he's in
need of a breather, or when he feels the game
has been getting on too well without him.

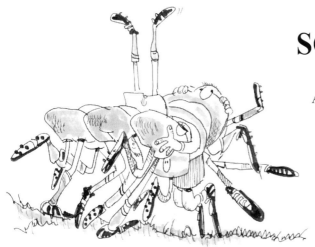

SCRUMMAGE

An organised group of forwards
from both sides with heads
down getting together to talk
about the inadequacies of their
backs or the ref.

LYING ON

A term used to describe a situation
when a player has about thirty players
on top of him and the ball below.

TACKLE

What happens when a player
without the ball can't get out of the
way of one who has.

DROP OUT

A typical ex-university, job-hunting,
third-XV centre.

RUCK

A term used to describe a punch-up when the ball is on the ground.

MAUL

Same as ruck punch-up, but when the ball and players are not on the ground.

PEEL OFF

The seconds at an after-match party.

BINDING

Stuff to hold your ears down.

BALL CARRIER

Chap in the crowd who sneaks off with it after it has been booted in there.

IN GOAL

The area between the try line and the dead-ball line where the grass is always lovely and green.

HOW TO AVOID TRAINING

Training is of course completely unnecessary, as any experienced player will tell you, but the trick is to make it look as if only the worst possible luck has stopped you from attending the training nights you want to attend so badly.

If you find yourself in such a dilemma (ie midweek training makes you too tired to play on Saturday) you may find the following suggestions of help.

PAY OFF THE COACH

This, though somewhat lacking in subtlety, can be very effective, as no coach (and any player will confirm this) can resist the sight of a tenner being proffered while you say something like "Look, coach – it's our wedding anniversary and the wife wants a little romantic dinner for two (wink here), know what I mean?"

His fat little grubby hand will instantly envelop the tenner as you rush back to the club to watch old international games on the big video-screen in the lounge.

AFRAID YOU'LL PEAK TOO SOON

This requires a degree of acting ability so we suggest it be tried by double-glazing salesmen, Jehovah's Witnesses or local politicians.

You are, of course, concerned about the team's performance, not your own, or so you say, and suggest that because of the high-tech progressive coaching that he, the coach, has subjected you to, you have hit your peak a few days too soon, and if he insists you train tonight you could be well over-peaked by match day. You'll happily train, you say, but he must bear the possible responsibility. He'll suggest you take a night off, of course - coaches are very sensitive about responsibility.

MID-WEEK TRAINING MAKES YOU TIRED FOR THE SATURDAY GAME

You can use this little gem only if (a) you are an indispensable member of the side or (b) if the coach hasn't already had a bet on the opposition for Saturday's game.

You simply say, "Sorry coach, I've wrestled with the problem, but if I train midweek I'm too tired to play on Saturday. The decision is yours, of course. I'll do whatever you want".

Coaches are, of course, afraid of decisions, and it'll be left to you. So you go back to the bar with the guy who's afraid he'll peak too soon, the floodlight-allergy guy and the one who's paid off the coach.

THE BANDAGED FOOT ROUTINE

This one never fails. You make a plaster of Paris cast which can be bandaged shut over a perfectly good leg. When you report on crutches on training night, you beg to be allowed onto the training ground. Your horrified coach stops you as you plead with tears in your eyes "The doctor had it plastered, it's not broken I'm sure". How could they then drop you from the side when you turn up miraculously cured ready for action on the match day muttering "Doctors, huh? What do they know?"

THE FLOODLIGHTS ALLERGY

This has to be used with caution and only if the training sessions are held under floodlights.

You explain to your harassed coach that if he's quite sure that the club's insurance policy covers your particular problem you're happy to train, but floodlights make you come out in a contagious rash which sometimes leaves men impotent. You support this with a story about your mother having a tragic affair with an electricity board fitter, at about the time you were born.

This works every time – you'll be banned from midweek under lights training forever. Coaches are dead scared of impotence.

HOW TO PLAY DIRTY

No matter what the purists say, now and again it is necessary to play a
"committed game" as it is referred to by the experts.

For the purposes of this chapter we shall refer to "committed" as good old-fashioned dirty.

The principle of playing dirty is by no means personal toward your opponent — it's also not
necessarily physical, just a means whereby you drain his confidence.

If you are reading this book to help you enjoy the game even from the touchline, it may
explain to you exactly what's going on out there. If on the other hand you are a player,
reading this wonderful book to help your game, feel free to use any of the following.

THE PAL-OF-THE-REF PLOY

This one is generally regarded to be a classic and again is simplicity itself . If executed with skill and timing, this play can guarantee you will have a great game — each member of the opposition being afraid to lay a finger on you.

All you do is say to the ref (whom you've probably never met before) "Don't forget, ref, I don't expect any favours from you — just because I saved your life in that boating accident". It works every time — the opposition will be afraid to touch you for fear of a penalty resulting every time.

THE SAS PLOY

This is guaranteed to frighten the life out of your opposite number and he won't come near you all match long.

Just look deeply into his eyes and smile as you dribble and make your one eye twitch as you say "I'm grateful for this chance. I didn't think the Rugby Union would let me ever play again after that business which led to them kicking me out of the SAS for being over-vigorous."

Try that one on as many as you can – you won't be troubled by them all afternoon.

THE BOOTLACE PLOY

This is a very tried and tested successful plan which irritates the chosen subject to such a degree that he runs around all afternoon with a fury that wrecks his whole contribution, yet the ploy is so simple.

If you see a pair of boots sticking out of a scrummage, whether the player is just pinned to the ground, having a rest or just good old-fashioned unconscious just tie the laces of his boots together. When he tries to get up he'll be furious — it works like a charm every time.

THE FROG PLOY

In this very cunning ploy you have to decide very early in the game who is their star scrummager.

As soon as the opportunity arises — ie when the star is pinned to the ground — shove a frog up his shorts or shirt. The panic that ensues ensures he'll think a lot before entering another scrummage.

THE MARTIAL ARTS PLOY

In the first line-out whisper to the opposing psychopath, "I think I should be fair and warn you — my hands are registered with the county police as dangerous weapons."

This always works because opposition psychopaths are invariably cowards in the face of real danger.

THE DIRTY WEEKEND PLOY

As you crush together in the warmth and dark of the very first scrummage quietly whisper in the opposition hooker's ear "One of our blokes spent last Easter with your missus when you were on that end-of-season tour of Italy."

This will ruin his concentration all afternoon — and his contribution to his team will be zero.

HOW TO LOOK LIKE A GREAT PLAYER.

There's nothing worse for making you look like an average player than for you to take the field in basic standard kit as supplied by your club.

If you really want to be noticed, you must exude an air of experienced ability. In order to achieve this, there are certain additions and alterations that you must make to your playing strip before you have the confidence to adopt the swagger that belies your playing inability.

THE SHIRT

Always doctor your shirt as soon as it is given to you. Cut through the stitching where sleeves meet shoulders so that at the first contact with the opposition they will tear — leaving you looking as if you have already been in the thick of the play.

Tearing the club badge or number on the back of the shirt half off is a nice touch too, as this lends an air of rebellious swashbuckling aggression, worth at least six points to your side.

THE SOCKS

Your socks should never, ever match your club jersey. Instead, they should be impressive Top Club socks (these can be bought from the Impressive Top Sock Shop at Twickenham). These socks alone will frighten your opposite number, who by now thinks you must be either a de-frocked All-Black or a struck-off Harlequin, even an ex-Bath or Cardiff player, and are secretly guesting.

Hypnotised by now, your opposite number doesn't even know you're an even worse player than he is until it's too late, and by this time your side's well in charge.

THE SHORTS

AS WORN BY WILL CARLING

Some cheapie clubs supply their players with soccer shorts, less expensive than rugby shorts, without pockets and waist-ties. Never ever wear these soccer shorts! You'll look like one of those fairies you see only in training videos and your career would come to an untimely end. With real rugby shorts being worn, you must always (when not actually involved in the game) thrust your hands deeply into the pockets of these shorts. It looks then as if you are thinking deeply about tactics — this always impresses the opposition, who are probably wearing cheap soccer shorts anyway.

Your shorts should also not be the same colour as the rest of the team. They should be bleach-faded blue, or dirty white — this gives the impression that you've been around a bit.

GUMSHIELDS

Unfortunately, the now common practice of wearing gumshields has partly put a stop to the old ploy of painting out a few teeth, enabling you to bestow a menacing smile on your opposite number. However, this can be achieved even when wearing gumshields by painting teeth on them, then blacking a few out again — you'll terrorise outside halves forever.

BANDAGES

You must always wear bandages with great subtlety. If you are a forward, go for the head bandage — always, of course, milky white — when you take the field. When you rise from the first scrummage with "blood" oozing through (via a punctured tomato sauce sachet), you glare angrily about you and you will be feared for the rest of the game.

Backs should wear the knee bandage, or thigh strapping. Both give the impression that you've played a bit and you are someone who's far too tough to allow such trivialities as torn muscles/hamstring tendons or the odd kneecap dropping off to stop you from getting at the opposition.

BOOTS

Boots are a give-away to the type of player you are, so remember
to prepare your boots well before kick-off.

There are three basic types of boot:

THE SPEED-MERCHANT BOOT

Even if these boots are brand new, you must tart them up. Iron the Day-Glo laces, highly
polish the toe caps so that when you are wearing them, with your hands
thrust deeply into your shorts pockets, (see previous chapter),
you run on the spot, click, click, clicking on the concrete
outside the opposition's dressing rooms.

This will give you an air of confidence and will make
the opposition think you are a speed merchant —
to be marked at all times — and you, being
deceptively slow on the pitch, will fool them yet again.

THE 'I'VE SEEN IT ALL BEFORE' BOOT

These are much loved by slow forwards. Your boots must look like
old campaigners, even if they are new. Scruff them up a
bit, bleach the toe caps, blood-stain the uppers,
throw out poncy Day-Glo laces and replace
that with old rope.

Once you have them on, use wide elastic
bandage to secure them. The macho effect is quite
extraordinary and inspirational — you'll play like a fading ex-international.

THE 'I'M-A-GONNA-MAKE-A YOU-AN-OFFER-YOU-CANNA-REFUSE' BOOT

This model is not readily acceptable in most clubs in this country, although
there are one or two Welsh Valley clubs that turn a blind eye, while clubs in
Italy readily and positively encourage them.

One thing these boots ensure — while wearing them, your
burst for the line isn't going to be impeded.

HOW TO ATTRACT THE ATTENTION OF SELECTORS

If you, dear reader, are still young and fit enough to still be playing or indeed are, because of this book, about to launch yourself into rugby, it's only natural that you wish for some sort of playing recognition.

Getting selected for the district/county/national sides has nothing to do with outstanding talent, as a quick look at any of those current sides will confirm. It has, however, everything to do with the skill of attracting the attention of the selectors and ensuring they remember your name.

Just imagine — it's probably the eighth game this week they've seen, so it's quite easy to attract their bored gaze away from the action, while you do something new. Soon your name will be remembered when they can't think of anyone else for a vacant representative position and once in the team, of course, you're there for ever, and as long as you're not a complete moron you will easily make the position your own. But first let us show you some ways of attracting the attention of selectors.

BLEED A LOT

There's nothing guaranteed to attract the attention of selectors more than a bleeding martyr. You collapse and feign unconsciousness. When revived, with blood pouring from a hairline wound (thinned tomato sauce) you refuse all efforts to be taken off for a blood injury. You make noises about wanting to die for your team etc etc.

You have to go off, of course, but on returning with head swathed in sauce-soaked bandages you play your heart out — often staggering around in an exhausted manner hoping to heighten the dramatic effect.

As the final whistle blows you collapse and allow team-mates to carry you off the pitch.

You may not have touched the ball all afternoon — but those selectors will never forget you.

DYE YOUR HAIR BLOND

English selectors are always suckers for this little ploy and it's so easy. All the would-be selected player has to do is to grow his hair long, and this done, dye it blond.

During the next game ensure you run about a lot (especially on the side of the field nearest to the selectors). Don't worry about the ball, just run about and if you can also shout things such as "We need this ball and I'm going blind side, chaps" it helps.

Properly executed this tactic will guarantee you're in the representative side before your dye bottle is half empty.

BE A PEACEMAKER

Selectors like seeing fearless players leaping in to stop ugly fights
without thought for their own safety.

The selectors (being basically simple minded) see this as an indication of the qualities
of leadership and fair play they desire in their side, and they'll probably think
you are also the type who likes to make after-dinner speeches as well.
So not only are you in the selected squad,
but probably as captain, too.

Stopping someone thumping the ref is
also good for attracting selectors —
but try to avoid doing this
as you risk the wrath of
the players.

MAKE SURE THE SELECTORS KNOW WHO YOU ARE

This necessitates you coming to a little arrangement (even financial) with whoever is in charge of the public address system to mention your name on every available successful occasion.

No matter who scores your side's points the crowd are told it's you. Ensure you get credit for tries, conversions, drop goals, penalties and carrying off injured opponents. Also make sure you're mentioned at half time for donating the ball.

When the selectors compliment you in the bar after about your game modestly say "Thank you, gentlemen I just hope I'm back to match fitness very soon" — as you press your name-emblazoned photograph into each selectorial hand.

WEAR A COLLEGE SCARF

Selectors are always a sucker for this one. Find out if any one of the selectors has ever been to university. If one has, buy the scarf of that establishment and wear that scarf — while playing!

This will be noticed and you will be pointed out as someone who is of superior intellect and mental notes will be made to select you as soon as possible.

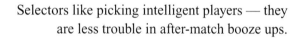

Selectors like picking intelligent players — they are less trouble in after-match booze ups.

NB: Don't use this ploy if you are a forward. Scarf-wearing forwards have been known to be strangled with the scarf by their opposite number.

NEVER BELIEVE AN EX-PLAYER

If you are a newcomer to the rugby scene you may be inclined to believe all the tales at the bar told by ex-players. International players in fact often make post-playing careers out of telling tales to anyone who offers to buy the next round.

You would be well advised, however, to remember that all ex-players embellish their stories in favour of themselves to improve the dramatic effect of the tale.

In short, ex-players are liars, so beware and look out for the following favourite tales.

"Of course I had several offers to go and play Rugby League".

What he failed to add was "mainly from my own team-mates".

"We were losing six-nil with five minutes to go. Our captain didn't have a clue, so someone had to take charge. 'This is what we do,' I said — and within a few minutes we'd put fourteen points on the board."

What he didn't mention was "The opposition also put another twenty one on the board".

"I knew he was good. Ex All Black, all muscle, bone and speed and nasty with it. I knew it was him or me, and I had to make my first tackle tell, so I was waiting for him and the first time he came running through like a wounded crazed bull I hit him as hard as I could — WHAM! That was it, I didn't see him again all afternoon."

This of course really means "I didn't regain consciousness until well after he and his team had gone back on their coach."

"Do you want to know why I didn't get a cap? I'll tell you. I told the chairman of selectors I wouldn't have him selecting our kids school side. I told him — he never forgot that"

While secretly he knows "I didn't get a cap really because I was rubbish!"

"So I told them, I did! Either the selection committee resigns or I leave the club."

He forgot to add "So I left the club".

"I side-stepped two players, handed off another three or four, then completely outpaced their defence as I sprinted fifty yards for the line".

This really means "I was a yard out hanging on to the ball and someone pushed me over the line."

"The crosswind was so strong I decided to place the ball rather than kick it out of my hands. I allowed correctly for the wind and bang it went sweetly through the posts."

What that really means is "I was trying
to boot it in near the corner flag.
The wind took it and we
had three lucky points."

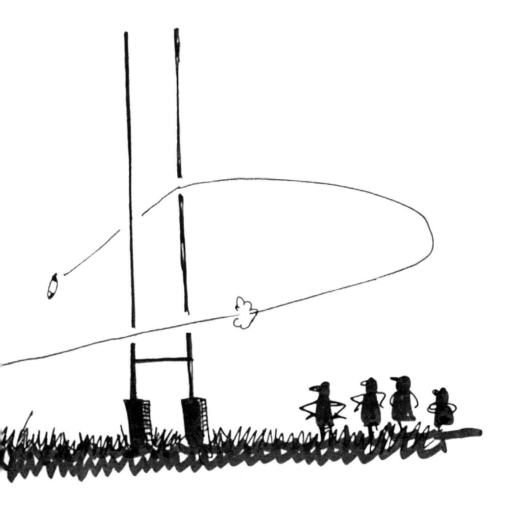

"I carried that club for years and when I left the club went to pieces".

This really means "When I left I took anything of value and the club's Easter tour beer kitty."

"What an Easter tour! Hundreds of raving rugby groupie girls hurling themselves at us."

Which means "Two girls at a bus stop waved at our coach as it passed."

REFEREES SIGNALS EXPLAINED

To enable players, spectators, the press and commentators to understand exactly what he's doing, the powers that be have established a series of referee's signals which should indicate exactly why he's ruining what could be a lovely, free-flowing game of rugby by generally making a nuisance of himself.

1. I'm totally confused,
but I know something
illegal happened

2. Do that to my son once
more and you're off, mate!

3. Hello Auntie

4. I saw the offence but he's too big for me to send off

5. I am the local hokey-cokey
champion

6. Don't expect me to run —
my guide dog bit me
yesterday

7. I have just penalised their vindictive psychopath

8. It's my first game and I am being sick

9. Please may I go
to the loo?

10. I am open to
cash bribes

11. My shorts have been ripped off

12. What the hell, it's my last game before I retire

HOW SUITED ARE YOU FOR A LIFE OF RUGBY?

To be a supporter, or a rugby player, you have to ensure that you are suited to the strange, sometimes even obsessively weird, ways of the Rugby World.

It would be wrong, therefore, to launch yourself into becoming a rugby type just because reading this wonderful book has encouraged you so to do.

At this point then, in this excellent yet remarkably reasonably priced book, we offer a test to see if you, dear reader, are ready for the Wonderful World of Rugby.

Question 1.

You are asked to turn out against a particularly nasty, unpleasant, All Blacks XV

Do you: A. Agree with pride to play?
           B. Pretend you're away on holiday?
           C. Resign from the club?

Question 2.

Your wife is about to give birth to your first child, and you have already planned to go with the club on their Easter tour of Devon.

Do you: A. Drop out of the tour?
           B. Phone her from Torquay if she delivers?
           C. Phone her from Torquay if she delivers and you win?

Question 3.

The man your wife deserted you for is propping directly opposite you.

Do you: A. Shake his hand and let bygones be bygones?
           B. Wait until the second half before you attempt to end his career?
           C. Get him in the first scrummage?

Question 4. **You are asked to stand on your rugby club committee.**

Are you: A. Proud to serve in any capacity?
           B. Proud to serve if you can claim expenses?
           C. Proud to serve if you can claim expenses and get all drinks free?

Question 5. **Your team is thrashed in an away game against your much-hated local rivals. During the after-match drinks at the bar,**

Do You: A. Compliment their team upon their play?
          B. Refuse to speak to any of them?
          C. Refuse to speak to any of them, but drink as much of their free beer as you can?

Question 6. **You are the captain, and you think the ref is having a terrible game.**

Do you: A. Express mild surprise at his interpretation of the laws?
         B. Call him a plonker when he's out of earshot?
         C. Get the plonker when he's not looking in the showers?

Question 7. **There's a sub-zero, force 10 gale blowing and the pitch is almost all under icy water.**

Do you: A. Demand vigorously that the game goes ahead?
B. Stay in the club bar?
C. Stay in the club bar watching blue movies?

Question 8. **Your club has had a large Sports Council grant. How would you suggest the money be spent?**

Would you: A. Propose the money be spent improving the club playing area?
B. Propose the money be spent enlarging the club bar?
C. Propose all members are given free beer until the grant is spent?

SCORING

Now, as a man with all the moral fibre that is required for a life in the world of rugby, it goes without saying that you will not cheat when adding up your scores.

Award yourself one point for each A
two points for each B
three points for each C

8-12 Points
Are you sure you're not a reject from a flower arranging group?

13-18 Points
With the help of this book, you could, with effort, become a rugby type.

18-24 Points
Congratulations, you're a natural — you're a real rugby man.

HOW TO BLUFF YOUR WAY THROUGH CLUBHOUSE CHAT

Once again dear reader, it could be that you are very new to this game and, as yet, feel slightly out of place when it comes to idle conversation at the club bar.

Do not be embarrassed with your lack of knowledge, because armed with just a few lines of intelligent conversational interjections, ready to be tossed in when the opportunity arises, you will soon be hailed as one of the club's "great thinkers of the game."

However, don't overdo it. You don't want anyone considering you for club chairman, do you?

Try to memorise some of the following and use them at will.

"Their scrum half was weak passing to his right — we should force him in that direction."

"We didn't take advantage of the fact that their outside half was very slow coming off his left foot."

"Those flankers just don't seem to compensate for each other, do they?"

"He was calling 19-23-26 when we really wanted more of a 19-11-10."

"We should have looped earlier to have released our overlap quicker."

"Remember how Van Der Pugh used that to great effect in the '74 Tour?"

"Frankly, I'd have played an outside half who isn't so predictable
and is much more committed to an expansive game."

"Why didn't we go left when their defence was
committed and exposed?"

"It was very obvious that their defence
was disorganised when it came
to our direct running."

IMPRESSIVE THINGS TO SHOUT FROM THE TOUCH LINE

Now that you have become considered a thinker by your club bar observations on the game, it's only natural that you will either want to, or be expected to, offer intelligent comments as you watch the game from the sidelines, or stand (depending on the standards of your chosen club).

Once more, you can be considered a deep-thinking expert by rehearsing some of the following comments and releasing them at poor unsuspecting players.

1. "You've got an advantage there, put the ball high into the sun."

2. "He's doing it again Ref - watch the binding this side"

4. "No, no, no, no. Full back! A counter
attack was on then, on
the short side"

7. "There, a
double reverse blindside
loop move on here, boys!"

5. "Watch the encroachment boys!"

8. "Where were you back row?"

6. "What's the matter Ref? Doesn't
law seven apply anymore?"

UNDERSTANDING THE COMMENTATOR

One of the great delights of watching rugby from the side-lines is the extreme pleasure we fans get from hurling verbal abuse at players as they perform their best on the rugby field.

Shouting at your star outside half something like "Yer playing like a geriatric one-legged fairy" is part of the real joy of being a loyal fan, but have you ever stopped to spare a thought for that much maligned group of rugby fans — the radio and TV commentators. They can't scream abuse at our sweaty friends can they? Well can they? Our research department has looked into this and have discovered that although the commentator may be unable to be as openly abusive as the touchline big mouth, even so they have their own albeit subtle ways of offering their opinions of some of the players. Experienced listeners have for years known what they really mean. For instance . . .

1. "**They play a very committed type of Rugby Football**"

They're the dirtiest bunch of thugs I've seen all season

2. "**The referee's interpretation of that law was interesting**"

I don't know what the hell the ref is supposed to be doing

3. "**They try to keep it tight up front**"

The backs are rubbish

4. "**They play an open running game**"

They're scared stiff to be tackled with the ball

5. "**His contribution often goes unnoticed**"

The ref should have sent him off in the first half

6. **"His tactical kicking often keeps him out of trouble"**
He can't pass

7. **"He plays with great tactical awareness"**
He's managed to avoid tackling anyone all afternoon

8. **"That's only the second time I've seen that tackle used"**
The first was during an SAS raid

9. **"He's a very underrated player"**
According to his mother

10. **"He's a great motivator"**
He's the big mouth of the team

11. **"He models his game on others"**
Like Attila the Hun

12. **"They're fielding an experimental team today"**
Half the Firsts are still drunk from last night

13. "They are a very sociable touring party"
Last night they were all as sociable as newts

14. "He's playing out of position today!"
He's rubbish and it's his last chance

15. "He's playing with a new-found confidence in his own ability"
The guy hoping to take over his spot has left the club

16. "He's made the position his own"
His father has just been made chairman of selectors

17. "His pace is deceiving"
He's much slower than you think

18. "He thinks about the game"
He doesn't do much else that I can see

19. "He had a season off from the game"
It would have been two but he got full remission

20. "He nearly got an international cap"
But the selectors wouldn't accept his bribe

THE RUGBY PRESS

Almost all rugby writers are ex-players (most of them are ex-internationals), while rugby writers on the quality Sunday papers are almost always ex-Lions. It's only natural, therefore, that because the writers and players are all palsy-walsy, the writers are not going to slate their friends, the players.

To protect this relationship, the writers disguise any criticism by using "purple prose", which can only be deciphered by those in the know. It seems only right therefore, that this wonderful volume should explain how the writers can say one friendly thing, but really mean another.

1. **"He's a good tourist"**
   He can apologise for his team's drunken binges in six languages, and plays the piano

2. **"His speed is deceptive"**
   Running fast makes him sick

3. **"His play is quite uncompromising"**
   He's broken his deputy's leg

4. **"I'm not quite sure they've read
the situation correctly"**
They should have got the dirty sod
in the first lineout

5. **"He's always there, or thereabouts"**
He's never actually got the ball

6. **"I feel he's sometimes playing out of position"**
Why doesn't he take up netball?

7. **"He took the more difficult option"**
The prat ran into their psychopath

8. **"The selectors seem to appreciate
the finer points of his game"**
I think he's rubbish

9. **"The score slightly flattered them"**
They were lucky to score anything

10. **"He's the thinker of the team"**
He's slow and clumsy

I PLAY RUGBY BECAUSE...

There are very many reasons why rugby is selected as the sport which claims the enthusiasm of so many.

Some of the reasons are not necessarily to do with a sporting desire or nature...

I like thumping people.

I like being in the showers with big hairy men.

I prefer rugby's more flattering hooped shirts to the ones soccer players wear.

I enjoy bawling obscenities in public.

My VAT man plays in the centre — I enjoy giving him hospital passes.

I don't enjoy the game at all but I really like getting drunk with the boys after.

I hope one day to be interviewed on Rugby Special.

I'll do anything to get away from the wife.

Twice a year I get a chance to get
that bloke who ran off with my wife.

I'm a touchline poseur. Its a
great way of pulling the birds.

TYPES OF RUGBY CLUB

If you are seriously thinking about joining a rugby club as a player or just a member, make sure you check out the club first.

For instance, it's no good joining one of those jolly clubs where each member is expected to turn out in the middle of winter to paint the stands, unblock the drains or mark and cut the pitch, if all you really want is somewhere to go for a quiet pint on a Sunday morning.

There are many clubs from which to choose, the following are the most usual.

THE SOCIAL CLIMBERS CLUB

If you wish to get on in the world, this is the club for you. The club goes back a hundred and fifty years and to even become considered as a member, you have to be recommended by someone who's at least a Freemason with an MBE, who's a friend of a local priest and, ideally, you should be related to the Chief Constable. Failing that, anyone who can pump a juicy sponsorship into the club.

Members of this type of club proudly flaunt their membership by wearing the club tie and scarf, always a garish combination of puce, mauve and orange stripes (designed many years ago by a colour-blind retired Malaysian rubber plantation manager), and the huge club badge, complete with Latin motto, worn wherever possible (ie blazer, shirts and boxer shorts).

The club's playing record is always dismal. This is always declared by the fumbling duffer making the speech at the club's annual dinner to be of no consequence, as the pride in representing such a great club is of far greater importance.

TACKLE ME IF YOU DARE, BUT I WARN YOU, MUMMY'S A GREAT FRIEND OF THE CHIEF CONSTABLE

THE PURELY SOCIAL CLUB

This club turned to playing rugby in the days when bars had to stop selling alcohol during the afternoon - so they had a game to pass those boring hours between stop and open tap. These days, what with much more relaxed licensing laws, only the last fifteen to get to the club bar on Saturdays have to play in the afternoon (the only law in the club's constitution).

Training is done around the club piano and the annual tour has nothing to do with a festival of rugby, but consists of regularly visiting breweries, distilleries or Continental vineyards.

THE CLUB THAT TAKES ITSELF TOO SERIOUSLY

This is the type of club that locks up the piano if the visiting team has won. Even top players are dropped if they fail to attend twice-weekly training sessions. The club proudly boasts a progressive youth policy, the club physiotherapist is not the usual struck-off vet and voting delegates are sent to the district or county AGM, always having been instructed which way to vote.

Always avoid this club, unless you have high HQ aspirations.

IN CONCLUSION

Well, dear reader, hasn't this book been of great benefit to you? Players will now know more of the art of retaliation. Fans will have learned to have become more vindictively eloquent. While the person who had always wanted to enter the world of rugby football, but didn't like to ask, will have a new-found air of confidence, as befits one who knows the difference between an over-committed player and one who's just a thug in rugby boots.

Here's to rugby, keep on rucking.

Thank you for buying this Western Mail & Echo Ltd publication. We hope you have enjoyed it, and as a special offer we have included this voucher giving 10% discount off your next book purchase.

Order any book from your local retailer or Western Mail & Echo Ltd and receive 10% off the R.R.P.

DISCOUNT

10%

This offer only applies to books published by Western Mail & Echo Ltd. However you may purchase your books from either Western Mail & Echo Ltd, or your local retailer.

Simply present this voucher when you purchase your next Western Mail & Echo Ltd book.

To the retailer: Complete the retailer coupon overleaf to claim your discount and send it back to the Book Department, Western Mail & Echo Ltd., Havelock St., Cardiff CF1 1XR. Wales, U.K.

RETAILER REDEMPTION COUPON

To the Retailer: Please accept this voucher as 10% discount off the R.R.P. of any Western Mail & Echo Ltd book. For a full refund of this 10% discount, please send this completed coupon to: **The Book Department, Western Mail & Echo Ltd., Thomson House, Havelock Street, Cardiff, CF1 1XR.**

When redeeming vouchers please ensure that all the details are completed. Only fully completed coupons are valid. No photocopies.

RETAILER DETAILS

Name ....

Address ....

....

Town ....

Post Code ....

Tel No. (daytime) ....

Contact name ....

PURCHASER/CUSTOMER DETAILS

Name ....

Address ....

....

Town ....

Post Code ....

Tel No. (daytime) ....

Book title purchased ....

R.R.P. ....

Discount given ....

POSTAL BOOK ORDER FORM ONLY

Order your next books by post for a 10% discount. This only applies to additional purchases.

To: **THE BOOK DEPARTMENT, WESTERN MAIL & ECHO Ltd.**
HAVELOCK STREET, CARDIFF CF1 1XR. S. GLAM. WALES

Please rush the following books to:
(Please print names and address CLEARLY)

Name ....

Address ....

....

Postcode .... Tel: ....

BOOK TITLE	ISBN No	**Qty**	***Price***	**Total**
Gren's Diary 1996	09504042 5X		**£5.95**	
Gren's Diary 1997 **Available Oct 96***	09504042 76		**£5.95**	
Gren's Guide To Rugby	09504042 68		**£4.95**	
Images of Cardiff	18598302 85		**£12.99**	
In the Footsteps of King Arthur	09504042 41		**£7.95**	
Total quantity/cost				
Special Discount Less 10%				
Add Postage & Packing @ £3 per book				
Total remittance enclosed				

Please debit my credit card

└┘└┘└┘└┘ └┘└┘└┘└┘ └┘└┘└┘└┘ └┘└┘└┘└┘ (expiry date) └┘└┘/└┘└┘

Name: .... Signature: ....
(CAPITALS)

Please allow 28 days for delivery on U.K. addresses or call into The Western Mail & Echo Offices in Cardiff.
Alternatively visit your local retailer.

Please note! Post and package applies to U.K. orders only, for overseas P&P add £10 per item.

CARTOON ORDER FORM

BOOK SALES DEPARTMENT

**Western Mail & Echo Ltd., Havelock Street,
Cardiff CF1 1XR. Telephone: 01222 583583**

For personalised and signed copies of your favourite Gren cartoons, please complete this form, not forgetting who your cartoon is for!

Size A4 (approx. 21x29cm / 8x11ins), printed on 160gsm buff matt art paper. Copy unframed.

Page Nº	Cartoon reference BLOCK CAPITALS PLEASE	Quantity @£8.00 ea.	Amount £
e.g. Page 11	THE PROPS NO.1 AND 3	1	£8.00
Postage & packing included to UK only. For overseas orders add £1.00. Alternatively orders can be collected from the Western Mail & Echo Ltd. at Thomson House. (Please allow 28 days for delivery in the UK)			
GRAND TOTAL	*Please enclose your remittance and make cheques payable to Western Mail & Echo Ltd*		

Your name & address

Name

Company Name

Address

Town

Post Code   Tel

Message . . . .

To ....

Best Wishes GREN

Please debit my credit card

⊔⊔⊔⊔   ⊔⊔⊔⊔   ⊔⊔⊔⊔   ⊔⊔⊔⊔   (expiry date) ⊔⊔/⊔⊔

Name: Signature:

(CAPITALS)   (PLEASE SIGN & SEND TO ABOVE ADDRESS)